OUT
OF THE
RAIN

An Anthology of
Drawings, Writings and Photography
by the Homeless of San Francisco

Compiled by Tom Fowler, Malcolm Garcia
and the Shelter Staff at the
St. Vincent de Paul Ozanam Shelter

St. Vincent de Paul Society of San Francisco

HUNT + GATHER
Bookseller & Publisher
311 Aztec St., Santa Fe
New Mexico 87501
@HuntAndGather.net

5-

Notice to unlocated authors:
This anthology contains the creative work of many current and former participants in the St. Vincent de Paul Society's and other organizations' shelter programs in San Francisco. The editors obtained this work from the individual creators over a period of many months, in all cases on the understanding that such work might be included in a publication of this sort. Unfortunately, for the very reasons the authors came to the shelters, *i.e.*, their homelessness and lack of a permanent address, and despite diligent efforts to locate each author, the St. Vincent de Paul Society has been unable to contact each and every contributor to this anthology for purposes of securing full consent to the use of his or her creative work. If your name appears as an author or artist herein, and you have not previously granted express consent to the use of your work in this book, the Society invites you to contact it at 1745 Folsom Street, San Francisco, California 94103.

Printed by Edwards Brothers, Inc.

Manufactured in the United States of America

Library of Congress Cataloging–in–Publication Data
Out of the rain : an anthology of drawings, writings, and photography
  by the homeless of San Francisco.
   p. cm.
ISBN 0-89407-141-6 (pbk.) :$9.95
   1. Homeless persons' writings, American—California--San Francisco.
2. Homelessness—Literary collections. 3. American literature--California—San
Francisco. 4. American literature--20th century 5. San Francisco (Calif.)—Literary
collections. 6. Homeless persons in art. I. St. Vincent de Paul Society of San Francisco.
PS508.H65O94 1988
810'.8'09206942--dc19   87-28888

ACKNOWLEDGMENTS

The St. Vincent de Paul Society of San Francisco wishes to thank the many individuals and organizations who have volunteered services, time, and monies toward this project. We apologize to any whom we may have inadvertently omitted from the following list, which is solely in alphabetical order.

Alphabetics

Jean-Louis Brindamour

Brobeck, Phleger & Harrison

Pam Brown

David Charlsen

Bill Chleboun

Sara Colms

Cragmont Publications

Bob Crooks

Elfrieda Fasal, M.D.

Fred E. Felder

Jim Foster

Tom Fowler

Jack Fronk

Malcolm Garcia

Thea Hamilton Gillette

Kathi Goldmark

Joe Hill

Harold Meyrowitz

Sylvia Morrison

Mark Muenter

John Murray

Melissa Mytinger

Jack Noonan

Northern California Book-sellers Association

Mike Painter

Jim Paulson

Christina Quiroz

Jerry Ricker

Nancy Ringler

Linda Sanders

Nick Setka

Bonnie Smetts

Balfour Smith

Wayne Strei

Julie Todd

Joe Wilson

When you're strange,
Faces come out of the rain,
When you're strange,
No one remembers your name,
When you're strange.

Jim Morrison—The Doors

Table of Contents

PREFACE

When we think of homeless people, we concentrate so fully on the tragedy of their situation that we often reduce them to pitiful objects huddled together on street corners rather than actual individuals possessing feelings, ideas, skills.

Out of the Rain is an attempt to move beyond this pathetic stereotype. The poems, letters, pictures, and photographs included in this collection reveal three–dimensional people existing on the fringes of our own lives. There is much pathos here, frequently colored with black humor. Structurally, many of the poems and pictures indicate a skill and education one would not expect of people too often and inaccurately depicted as "shiftless" and "lazy".

It is our hope that *Out of the Rain* will show its readers something of the character and lives behind the flat portraits we frequently see but rarely are compelled to consider.

Malcolm Garcia

INTRODUCTION

St. Vincent de Paul Society social worker Tom Fowler and I had long been aware of the artistic talents of many of the users of the Society's shelter. Snooping over hunched shoulders, picking up crumpled sheets of paper, we saw work that had obviously required time and thought to write, rewrite, and rewrite yet again—to draw, re–draw, and draw yet again—work that finally resulted in thoughtful, provocative pieces from the human drama.

> *The faces I see*
> *When I come here*
> *Remind me of where I came*

We knew it would be unrealistic to expect the homeless to commercially pursue their artistic talent; with the daily search for shelter, work and food, how would they find the time and money to submit their work for publication, and what addresses could they give on their stamped, self–addressed return envelopes?

> *Living life's everyday grind*
> *Is enough to blow your mind*

So Tom and I decided to provide a means, if they would provide the materials. From August, 1986, through April, 1987, we collected countless sketches and poems, as well as a few short stories and photographs. Then we had to decide the criteria for the work that would actually appear in the proposed collection.

Work that through words or pictures depicted real people, real situations, even though possibly foreign to our own experiences but believable, honest, compelling, received a strong nod from us.

> *She was thin enough to call skinny,*
> *tall, angular and I thought a strong*
> *wind might blow her away.*

Subtlety of approach was another consideration. To read the words, consider a picture with immediate understanding yet haunted, made slightly uncomfortable, so we returned again and again for the meaning between the lines, shaded gray in the shadows, not easily apparent but accessible with thoughtful inquiry and consideration.

> *We Walk Empty Streets Looking For Schemes*
> *Most Times A Doorway Our Bed*
> *It Seems We Could Lay There Forever And Ever*
> *Then Briefcases March Thru Our Dreams.*

Is the "Crazy Woman with Pet Dead Pigeon" really crazy? What had she once cradled in her crooked arm? What about "In This Bottle of Wine?" It provides word pictures to describe the destructively secure grip the narrator has with his bottle of wine.

So have another drink to the memories
And two more drinks to forget.

Out of the rain, out of the doorways, out of "everyday's grind," come stories, poems, sketches and photographs that testify to the infinite resiliency of the human spirit and its ability to see and to speak creatively no matter what the condition of life.

J. Malcolm Garcia
Director, Tenderloin Self–Help Center

TONY'S CART

A STRANGER IN YOUR LAND

Walking down the city sidewalks
Contemplating the rain
Lost in thought on this dreary day
Should be in bed anyway
Time is running But you don't really know
The sand is shifting away
People rushing here and there
They never hear what you say
You feel like a stranger in
Your own land
Sometimes reality is out of your hands
You're a stranger in your land

Catch a cable car down to the wharf
The San Francisco Bay
Sit on the pier drinking a beer
The world it feels all right
And then you get up and turn around
You look the city in the eyes
It's an animal stalking you
Flowing in with the tide
You feel like a stranger in
Your own land
Sometimes reality is out of your hands
You're a stranger in your land

The city makes you small
It's a feeling you see
It's as mad as a rabid dog
Running loose in the streets
No one here knows your name
They wouldn't if they could
Everybody runs their own way
Like good strangers should
You feel like a stranger in your own land
Sometimes reality is out of your hands
You're a stranger in your land

Champ Means

CONVERSATIONS

WHERE SHOULD I START? I guess I should go back to where I can remember. I can't really remember past six years old and then it is kind of hazy of what my life was about. I can recall when my uncle used to baby sit with us kids. I always thought he was a little crazy myself. He also had sex relations with me and I guess I'll always remember that I used to run and hide in the bushes after that happened. He told me never to tell anyone cause if I did, I would be punished and God would put me in hell, big Deal. I didn't have to worry about that because I put myself there already. I was really glad when he died I should be ashamed of myself for being that way but I'm not. I went to school when ever my father pushed the issue other wise I played hookey more than I went. The Kids always made fun of me because I was so shy in school with my work, I'd have to cheat and write my answers on my hand where I had remembered the answers at the time so I wouldn't forget them and the principal always said that I had cheated by looking at other peoples paper, but it wasn't true it's just that I was not good at remembering things it was very hard for me. I'll bet we were the only kids in town to go through a different baby sitter every week. I guess us kids weren't exactly the best kids around we always did what we wanted well usually. My sister got jealous once when her girl friend became better friends with me then with her and she tried to hang Marsie in our tree in our back yard we got Marsie out of the tree in time to see Nancy set fire to the back of the House. Boy did she ever get beaten when Mom and Dad got home from work.

Actually, I always thought it was funny when she got in trouble because she always hid things better than me. She always had more friends than I did. But I guess I was meant to be alone. I remember when Marsie and I lived across the street from each other we were always the best of friends. I just wish we still were because I miss her friendship very much. Anyway when we were 11 (me) and 10 (her) there was a boy that lived on the same block as us we couldn't stand him or for that matter his mother (which also had an alcohol problem). He was always throwing things at us and calling us stupid names But we got even with him. We made him a Mud pie out of a Sewar and made him eat it, oh, what fun that was, until he told his mother which in turn told our mothers which in turn beat our asses and wouldn't let us play together for a week they thought. But we managed to still see each other they weren't really as smart as they thought they were because her mom and my mom always went to the bars together and we were always in trouble doing things together but at that age we didn't care. Mom and Dad always threw beer parties and they'd always let us kids have Booze they really didn't care about our drinking. But we all nearly got beat to death when we were discovering what each other's body was like, because Mom and Dad didn't have time to tell us the facts of life, so we figured we'd find out ourselves which believe me was a bad mistake. We lived on 9th Street for a long time and I had another girl friend which at the time I was fifteen years old and I really had a crush on her brother which was eighteen and I thought he was the nicest guy I had ever met. He was so kind and nice to me and he even took me on dates to the show and

Dinner it was really nice. I Hurt so bad when he was killed in a boating accident. We were all out on the Missouri River in his boat when it snagged something and turned over. He saved three of us girls but went under and when he tried to come back up he came too close to the motor on the boat—it really was a horrible sight. It was very hard to get over. I spent two months in the Hospital they said I had a nervous breakdown after it happened. I don't remember much about that. I started hanging out more and more in bars after that, it was my Dumb idea to go out on the River. I guess I'm to blame for what happened. I had always went to the bars with my Grandma and mother since I was 11, but then I started going by myself. I used to know some of the hookers and they would line me up with dates for $5.00 and maybe $10.00 it kept me in booze. I have gone out with so many men that I couldn't count How many in my life and at times I didn't know who, or what they looked like. I knew that I was meant not to have anyone to love and care for. I have lived in so many places and lost so many friends over my drinking I even sold myself for a quarter at one time. When I was eighteen years old I used to walk the streets because my Parents and I just didn't never get along any more. I think they preferred I didn't ever come home. I tried to get their Love and attention by trying suicide, oh, they really noticed. She had me locked up for what seemed like such a long time finally it got where I didn't really care what happened to me. I was Raped and Dragged off the Streets in a car by a bunch of boys. I tried to have someone help me but it was real late and I had just come out of the show (believe it or not I was sober) one of my moments when I needed a show instead of a drink. I Had these moments quite a bit, no one saw or cared, often they brought me back to town they threatened and said for me not to tell anyone or they would come back and Kill me which at the time really scared me. The only person I told was my girl friend Elaine and she said it was probly the best I Forget it (I Haven't). I used to go to the Record Hops and I had a good time, too. I never drank and didn't want to when they had them I didn't care back then about drinking. I have liked a lot of Guys but it seems all the good Guys I cared about always ended up either getting killed or dying from some kind of disease. I love to go for walks when it is storming I've always felt at peace with my self going for Walks by my self when its bad weather. I used to sleep in Parks, by my self and was never afraid of any thing. I miss all of my family which consists of my uncle, my Grandmother (which I adored and Loved more than my Mother), my mother, my Grandfather, my aunt and uncles. I Loved them all and have none of them left except for one Uncle that can go to Hell.

Anonymous

THE BEVELED EDGE

Oh sadness, sadness beyond madness
    What have you brought me, God?
Can it be that all this pain
    was some peculiar sort of education?
Can it be those enticing pleasures
    were but a trickster's delight?

I know and you know too,
    that we've got some sort of thing here—together
Let it be, for once, untrammeled
    unaborted, unflappable
And as always, nearly unbelieveable.

Morris Peltz

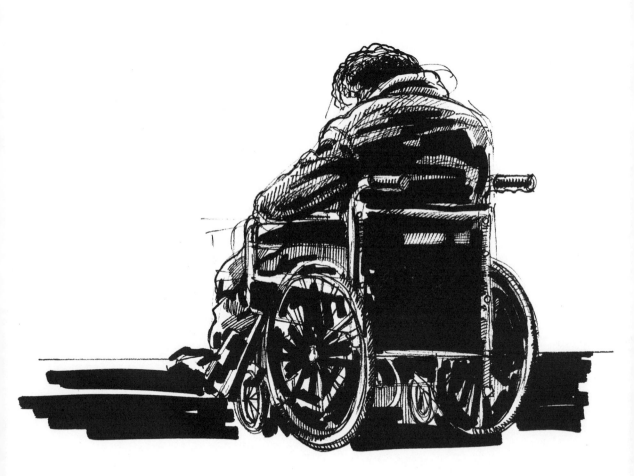

FROM WHERE I CAME

The faces I see
When I come here
Remind me of where I came
And the things I fear

People lost deep inside
Not knowing where to go
The confusions and feelings
I only too well know

All these people
As down as they are
Aer what I use
As a guiding star

So, I'll always try
To remember my true aim
And never forget this is
From where I came

Mr. Mike

S Rowe '85

UNTITLED

At once,
The will is strong
The man is up
And toward the store
Seen the will decline
And he is up
To get some more
Until the silver money flows
Like water
Through his hands
And the castle of his soul
Is built
Upon alcoholic sands

K. Kern

BACK TO FLORIDA

I WAS GOING BACK TO FLORIDA; just as soon as my check was forwarded from Acton, a Los Angeles County "drunk farm" to Venice's CLARE Foundation, I'd get it cashed, hop a local bus out to L.A.'s International Airport, and be gone.

For days I'd been sleeping under Lincoln Boulevard, overlooking the Santa Monica Freeway, but sleeping under bridges was nothing new to me. I wouldn't have broadcast to the public rolling overhead all night that I was there, and had hundreds of cash dollars in my dungaree pants pockets, but as it was, I wasn't too concerned.

I was glad I hadn't made more definite plans because by the time that second check I'd been waiting for finally did catch up to me, I was about out of money and almost in immediate need of it. I'd been spending freely, nearly four months out of practice at managing a pocket full of cash; momentarily expecting the check that would replenish my dwindling resources. I was running days behind my earlier roughly planned schedule, but I thought to myself, who's on a schedule? Certainly not me. I knew that I'd follow my normal standard procedure, and get there whenever I happened to get there.

I made a phone call when I finally got out to "LAX." I called my mom in Florida. "Yeah, Mom, I'm still in California—I know it's been weeks, I'm sorry—Ma, I should be in Florida in a couple of hours."

"Hey, Ma, I don't care what you heard on the radio! So, the tourists are flockin' to Florida; I'm flying."

I hadn't been in Florida in over a year, and hadn't spoken to my mother in a few months. The last she knew, I was up in the mountains of southern California at Acton. She's never been as far west as the Mississippi River, but she knew where her son was. And that he'd been living out in California for over three months. She also knew that I moved fast, so it only blew her mind momentarily when I made the sudden announcement that I was on my way.

After I hung up, my next stop was the United Airlines window where I held up two crisp C–notes, and asked when the next flight would depart for Tampa, Florida.

I wasn't concerned what airline I flew, or even with the flight's exact destination. I realized there wouldn't be more than a few dollars difference, and all I wanted was a quick trip to Florida.

"Well..." the studious young ticket agent sounded doubtful. "The next flight to Tampa will be taking off in about an hour and twenty minutes, sir—"

"Good," I smiled, relieved and thankful.

"—but, I'm afraid it's sold out."

"What do you mean, sold out?" I answered angrily. "Are you telling me that there's not a seat available?"

Her head shock negatively. "I'm sorry, sir..." She smiled nervously.

"On the whole damned airplane!" I laughed.

"I'm sorry, sir—"

"Don't be sorry!" I snapped, suddenly angry. "Sell me a ticket!" I waved the two hundred dollar bills at her.

"If I can't go to Tampa, I guess I'll have to settle for Miami," I said in disgust, not looking forward to the long trip across the Tamiami Trail, or Alligator Alley, or whatever the hell I'd hitchhike across the state when I got there, but at least I'd be in Florida.

"Miami was sold out before Tampa," she continued apologetically.

I laughed again. "What would you suggest?" I asked, for the first time becoming fearful about making Florida today.

"Now...?" She was dumbfounded.

"Now!" I growled menacingly. She saw six foot, three inches, a hundred–and–eighty–five pounds, and ice blue eyes staring at her through long, shaggy hair and a dark, scruffy beard; then she started beating the hell out of her computer!

While she did, I recalled and calculated from a mental map, offering, "Atlanta?" I knew that Atlanta was three times as far from Tampa as Miami was, but I was getting desperate.

"It's Easter weekend..." she feebly informed me as she madly punched buttons on the computer console before her.

May Frankie Avalon and Annette Funichello both drop dead, I thought, recalling Fort Lauderdale and their "Spring Break" pictures.

"Atlanta's sold out, too," she said as she shrunk back fearfully. She looked like she might be thinking about my coming over the counter and physically attacking her.

"What...?" I said. Where, I wondered. Where can I go?

"You know," she said, throwing up her hands in defeat. "I couldn't get you to New York, if you wanted to go..."

"I don't want to go to New York, anyway," I said angrily.

I was really annoyed by this time, but I was trying to maintain my cool. I had the money, and I wanted to go to Florida; I wanted to go home.

But this "sweet" young woman wouldn't let me. "Say something, girl! What's going where?"

Slowly, she turned around, searching for a way out.

I was no longer angry; I was tired. I just wanted to sit down and have a couple of drinks.

The gate was right behind her, so she read the sign. "The Hawaiian Express should already be gone; its flight to Honolulu is ten minutes late now," she said for lack of anything better.

"Gimme a ticket!"

"No, are you sure?"

"Positive!"

"But," she started writing, "but, where's your luggage?" she said as I grabbed the ticket.

"In Hawaii," I laughed over my shoulder as a I strode down the ramp.

A few hours later, I telephoned my poor mother in Florida. "Hi, Ron!" she said happily. "Where are you?"

"Honolulu."

"Huh?"

Ronnie Finch

DESOLATION

A foghorn deep unseen,
behind a pastel wall
inside a void of impenetrable fog;
A wintry summer breeze
inside the private world
that contains my misty loneliness.

The roar and splash of waves,
upon an empty beach
fronts my facade of solitary smiles;
The mournful cry of gulls
upon the cold damp air
contains the empty shell
of my spirit.

The long brick passage
lined by columns of amber lights
is cavernous and empty,
Inside the city flanked by traffic sounds,
People going home to loved ones
and their warmth,
while I have this vacant concourse
all to myself.

Seth Richardson

THE JIVE BITCH WITH THE POOL STICK

I was standing around
In the heart of town
With nothing much to do
So I smoked a joint and ate some lunch
And decided to shoot some pool
I went into the pool hall looking for a game
When I checked out this chick claiming her fame
She was a cute little lady with medium brown hair
A jive talkin' bitch but her game was fair
The game was snooker and the score was tied
Then she banked the five ball, three rails in the side
She ordered a beer as she studied the six
Then she cut it in the corner with smooth stroke of the stick
The guy she was playing decided he'd quit
He'd lost four games straight to this jive bitch with the pool stick
So I stepped into the scene with a zebra wood cue
And I asked the little lady if she's like to shoot a few
She said sure pretty little papa you don't look so tough
So I gathered the balls and racked them up
We played from six that evening until four the next morning
I was six hundred ahead and the game was getting boring
One final game I said as I caught her counting her bread
And looked around the room. Then double of nothing, she said and smiled
But all the while her heart was filled with gloom
Well, it didn't take long before the game was done
And the little lady was all out of money. So I scratched my crotch,
Looked at my watch, and asked how about some breakfast, honey?

Weldon Kennedy

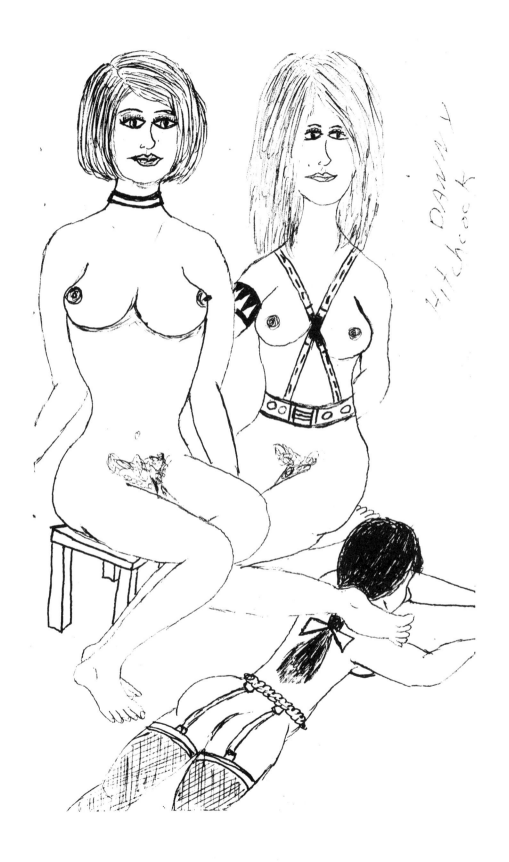

MYRTLE AVENUE

FIVE BOYS CAGED TWELVE PIGEONS for a week without food. Then one of the boys carried the pigeons up to the roof of a burned out apartment building in the Projects while the four remaining boys scattered pieces of stale bread in the middle of Myrtle Avenue. When the birds were released, the boys on the Avenue crouched, circling, leaping into Bruce Lee *Enter The Dragon* kicks and Chuck Norris *A Force of One* kicks as the pigeons dove for the food. They kicked them before they landed and the whole thing grew very loud and amid the flutter of lightly descending feathers, distorted faces shoved out of open windows snarling for quiet. It rained the following morning but in the afternoon the rain stopped and it got very steamy outside and the stink from the Avenue was practically intolerable.

Anonymous

CRAZY WOMAN
WITH PET DEAD
PIGEON

UNTITLED

Inner light
Blinding
A beaming ray of truth
To one in middle years
With the shadow of his youth
Not quite yet distorted
With
The gin and the vermouth
A thread
More like a wire
That binds the sacred
With the uncouth

K. Kern

SYRUP SWEET

Syrup sweet,
    thrift, thrift
        white or wheat
    wheat, wheat

Syrup, erupt, erupt, erupt
    thrift, thrift
        white or wheat, white or wheat
    wheat, wheat, wheat, wheat, wheat

Syrup sweet,
    thrift, thrift
        white or wheat
    wheat, wheat

Syrup, erupt, erupt, erupt
    thrift, thrift
        white or wheat, white or wheat
    wheat, wheat, wheat, wheat, wheat

Anonymous

SNAP, CRACKLE, POP

Snap, Crackle, Pop
The Jewish Be–Bop

Slip, Slop, Hop
When the somersaults stop

Act Doozy—Be Boozy
There are no somersaults
When one is woozy.

Michael David Wilson

I GIVE UP

I give up! I give up! I give up!
    I'm really fucked and
    there's no point more
    to further playing.

Aren't you overdoing it a bit?

Hell, no, baby, I'm just getting started.
    I'm going to get so humble
    that, barring none,
    I'm going to humiliate God into action,
    or out of his inaction.

Fat chance, you have!

Risk always measures challenge.

Morris Peltz

WALKING IN CALIFORNIA

Walking in California
saw some people easing back
and not giving a damn
because they'd nothing to give a damn about
just getting by with occasional smiles
and paying the bills

Walking in California
saw some people who were activists
and they were crying out
against some things no one else knew happened
naming some fish and a kind of bird
and crying real tears

Walking in California
saw some people on the street
and wearing their hunger
while the warm and fed looked beyond them
too busy scurrying ahead
and making ends meet

Walking in California
saw some people preaching God
and bearing their crosses
to condemn the laughter of mankind
forecasting dark at the end of the tunnel
and helping themselves

Walking in California
saw some people singing songs
and not giving a damn
because they'd nothing to give a damn about
just getting by with occasional smiles
and paying the bills.

Seth Richardson

IT'S ON YOU OR MAYBE ON HIM

Does man propose and God dispose?
      I think so
      But can't tell you exactly why.

I have witnessed a miracle or two
      In my day but
      They may yet be explained
      By as yet unknown scientific formulae.

Is this God a person or some Autonomic Force
      Operating within and around us?
      I wish I knew.

Still, we must choose to act credibly!
      To reconcile virtue and impulse,
      Freedom and duty,
      Dignity and desire.

Words come so easily,
      I hardly know
      If honorable acts ensue.

Morris Peltz

SORROW

Sorrow is the only faithful one
Clean like a season without any reason
Sorrow is like the spy who has to lie, cheat, and manipulate
Or he'll die.
Sorrow is like the load that's too much to tow
With your mind feeling like it's going to explode
Yes, sorrow is the only faithful one.

James English

WAITING FOR A BED IN DETOX

A BOTTLE OF WINE

Me and my wine, we just lay here
And sometimes one of us can stand

Once in awhile we'll try to remember
The things we've spent years to forget

Like the wife who forgot it was
Death do us part
Took the car and the kids
And forsaked us

Or the girl that we met
She couldn't help our regrets
For leaving a life far behind us

So have another drink to the memories
And two more drinks to forget

Now lovers and friends all come in a bottle
And sometimes there's room for a pet

In this bottle of wine
Flows the life that we live
So don't pour me out on the streets

Yeah, me and my wine
We just lay here
And sometimes one of us can stand

We walk empty streets looking for schemes
Most times a doorway's our bed
It seems we could lay there forever and ever
Then briefcases march through our dreams

So have another drink to the memories
And two more drinks to forget
I'll tell you of yesterday's ambitions and plans
But the blackness of night fills my head

Yeah, me and my wine we just lay here
And sometimes one of us can stand
If this life that we lead
Seems strange to some
And our travelin' gear awful light
Why, me and my wine we seldom complain
When the rain and stars fall upon us

So have another drink to the memories
And two more drinks to forget

We've got a ticket to hell
On the night train express
But the whistle
         sounds
            far
                down
                    the
                        track ...

Conrad

CONVERSATIONS

CHARLIE AND I FINALLY STARTED GETTING ON FRIENDLIER TERMS; we played cards quite a bit, but every time I beat him at rummy he'd call me a bitch and get up and leave—must have been a sore loser.

Well, we decided one day that we wanted to go to the show, which you are supposed to get permission for first, which of course we never did, but went anyway.

Ran into a counselor at the show but he promised not to tell on us. We got back in time when the people were getting back from AA, so we got to go in with them, otherwise we would have been locked out. I've been locked in them places before, but never locked out, I should have gone on back downtown, but they would have just sent the police after me and we really never got along together.

I remember when Mom and I got into it and I slapped her. She sent me away from the house and told me not to come back until I could show her some better respect. Ha, Ha! That would be the day. I took off for the Silver Dollar, King's Row and Tom's Place. I got so wiped out that I woke up at my girlfriend's house, not knowing how I got there, but I didn't care because I didn't want to go home anyway. I stayed away from there for a month, at the time my brother was on the police force, a fuckin cop—God!

Anyway, one night Dorothy and Bob were watching TV and she called my attention to the news, that the police were dragging the river for a body that had been seen in it, and Mom was on TV telling them she was sure it was me, because I had told her so many times that if she didn't leave me alone, that I would kill myself. Now, really, do I look the type? I like life at times, not always, but most of the time. Anyway, Dorothy said I had to call Mom and let her know I was o.k. or I would have to leave, so I left. Let her worry, I didn't care. Just my dumb luck, it was snowing like a bitch and I had no shoes to wear so I had to leave barefooted, not bad after your feet get used to the cold snow. The police picked me up, asked me if my feet were cold, so I told them where they could go. Went to the station (which grew to be my home, the biggest part of my life). They called and told Mom I was alright and for her to come down and get me (so touching). At the age of 21 yet. Well, I decided to jump out the window, which was on the second floor, so naturally I missed the ground and hit the cement, a broken back was the result. Boy, when I fuck up I do it right.

I made front page, picture and all. Not much good for the Police Department, but they wrote me up pretty good. Two months spent there, and the doctors and nurses were always trying to get me to move into a room with other patients. I told them I was keeping my private room, I couldn't stand lying around nice, nosey people. I preferred being by myself. I was always a loner,and will probably remain one.

Anonymous

SRowe 186-85

JUDGE ME NOT

Judge me not
For who is to say what is right or wrong
For who is to say what is fast or slow
For who is to say do this or that
For who is to say don't do this or don't do that
No one has the right to say
What to do or not to do
Because living life's everyday grind
Is enough to blow your mind
Life is the music—everyone dances to it
So judge me not
For I am only dancing to the rhythm
Of my life's beat.

James English

HUSTLERS AND MOOCHERS

I don't mind a good con job,
    if only it paid enough.

But for how much can one sell oneself:
    (1) a prayer
    (2) a kiss
    (3) a punch
    (4) salvation
    or just mere money.

Mooching, on the other hand, is delicious.
    Goodies all over the place.
    Tastes to every delight—
    A phantasied nothingness.

Oh, God, give me the election to mooch
    and not hustle!

Oh, Man, give the credit for indecision.

Morris Peltz

PLAYING SPADES

FOR A WAITRESS

fatty meat on a dirty grill,
crazy neighbor bitches,
"books, no room!"

closed for vacation—
they don't know what they're
talking about.
still, jamacian gold tooth
flashes happy wisdom.

Roberta D'Alois

UNTITLED

They are undercover agents
pretending to be good advice.
They are provocateurs against lucidity.
They are not nice.
They use any style to convince.
Their evidence is marred;
they cover their own fingerprints.

They even use facts as a deflection.
They are myopic.
They would escape apprehension.
They would change the topic.
They hide behind the flag
or revolution's banners.
With their civil servant's care
and drag queen's manners
they plant bombs anywhere.

Invoking any claim,
they blow love to hell.
They are insane.
In our common pain
they would stop us
from our considered choosing.
They would confine us
with their idea of protection.

Of course, we do need help.
We are fooled as much as we accept them
as ordinary in our lives.
When we look
their pretense is always revealing.
When we love
we are all uncovered in our feeling.

Michael Porter

AGNOSTICS

Every man has a right to be an agnostic.
Agnostics are not dependent on us.
We are dependent on them.
Agnostics do not believe in God.
They come from Missouri.
Agnostics do not live in the days of the Saints.
They live in the days of the Aints.
Agnostics say "Donde Dios?"
There are Hindus and Buddhists and Jews
and Moslems and Catholics and Christians
who know all the answers.
Agnostics say "Today, where is God?"

Anonymous

ABANDONED

Abandoned by my family at the age of eight
And put behind a big, strong gate
At the age of eight I learned to hate
And stayed in that grind for a very long time
At the age of 23 I began to see
A brand new world in store for me
I've always had the yearning for learning
If this yearning for learning doesn't stop burning
Maybe some day I'll be able to say
I spent the best part of my life in the most beautiful way

James English

LIVING IN YOUR WORLD AND HITTING THE TOP

LIVING IN THIS WORLD FOR SO MANY YEARS and trying to get on my feet is like climbing a mountain and slowly. So I'm climbing day and night on till I get tired then take a rest that same night, night past that one day and morning is here. Start to climb again higher and higher. I look far up, wonderfing if I'm going to make it to the top. So I'm climbing and climbing on till I get halfway; then when I'm halfway there, I slip and fall. It was a painful fall at that, so I rested that day and the next day I start climbing. The second day passed and I rested, night is gone and morning is here. On the third day, I'm climbing and climbing, higher and higher, and knowing I'm going to make it is half the battle.

And finally I'm getting closer and closer. On that night I rested. The following morning I climb like nothing is going to push me down and on that very same day I grab the top and push myself up and nothing in hell is going to make me climb down.

Larry M.

I GOT YOU UNDER MY SKIN

"I got you under my skin"
Young women are not
Your sin
Make lust your friend
And accept your end
Bend your mind and swing your hips
And be ready for another ship

Michael David Wilson

PRETTY HANDSOME, YOU THINK IMPORTANT

I'm not vain, it's true
    but I think I know
    my own worth.

The truth is simple:
    I'm not the handsomest guy in town;
    I'm not the ugliest.
    I'm not the richest boy on the block;
    But I'm not the poorest.

The fact is that I'm simply the
    nicest guy you ever will meet!
    I pay attention.
    I show concern and
    I really care.

What more can you really want?

After all, moral prettiness has its own glow.

Morris Peltz

WHERE AM I NOW?

Where am I now, and
what to meet—the wicked
City's vilest street.
Dark looks upon me are
thrust and lo, the ope
the accursed door and
I must go, I know I must.

P. Jones

OLD CLOTHES IN A CLOSET

I woke up this morning
    feeling like her husband
        once again.
Strange how some kinds of time
    fly bye
And other times
    stand still
Like old clothes
    in a closet
You open the door
    and the memories hang there
No longer in fashion
    but nevertheless
        irreplaceable.

Conrad

WAITING FOR COFFEE

TO WISH AND NOT WISH

I wish that I had never bothered
    To want all those things
    I either never got,
    Or, having gotten,
    Soon ceased to care for.

Whatever perplexity mere want assumes
    Hardly reduces the simplicity
    Of knowing that, for once and all,
    Desire, itself, is a fickle matter,
    Never to be trusted,
    Nor yet ousted from its primacy.

What not not wish?
    Surrender the vagary of phantasy.
    Upend the slender reed of intention.
    Put off hope and delay anticipation
    All this to retire volition.

Can we ban wishing?
    Is it either healthy or legal
    To moon around,
    Pretending to capture the essence of life
    By mindless, palaverous phantasizing?

How hard we can be on ourselves
    Masking our dogged impulse
    To hide from all and ourselves
    The plain fact
    That to see and care
    Is to feel and want.

I give up!
    I want much more than I can ever get.
    I can really handle much less than I can ever receive.
    To wish or not wish is irrelevant.
    Only living and dying measure the true reality.

Morris Peltz

MISS T.

IT WAS THE FIRST DAY OF SCHOOL, seventh period. Our schedules read, "English, Miss Thermohlen, Room 209." As Mike and I sauntered into the rapidly filling classroom, we grabbed the only two side–by–side empty desks in sight. They weren't directly in front of the teacher, but I thought they were too damned close for comfort.

A trim, light–brown–haired young woman sat at her desk facing the class. There were three stacks of text books beside her, and she appeared to be engrossed in one of them.

We suspiciously eyed her, as I'm sure she expected, and I noted that she had freckles, but I thought they hardly belonged. Freckles go with a short, solid, well–rounded figure, and she was none of these. She was thin enough to call skinny, tall, angular, and I thought that a strong wind might blow her away. her hair was long, thing, and straight. Mousy?

"THERMOHLEN" was boldly printed on the blackboard.

"Hey, Mike," I whispered, "How would you pronounce that name?"

"Termite," he shot back.

I tried to conceal a laugh, but couldn't entirely, as the class looked at us, a pair of cutups, wondering what they'd missed.

Fearing the possible loss of control of the class so early in the game, she immediately took evasive action.

As a group of young high school kids, we never realized that in reality, this woman's entire future hung on her initial control of our class. (And, if we'd ever had such realizations, we wouldn't have given a damn.)

She hadn't heard what was said, but she was aware it was in reference to her, so she quickly got to her feet, faced the class with a "no nonsense" expression, and said with a very British accent, "Good afternoon class." She only had to wait a moment for silence, then she continued. "My name is," she pointed at the blackboard, then clearly and distinctly said, "Miss Thermohlen."

"How do you say that, Mike?" I whispered again.

"Termite!" That was a loud whisper, I thought, as giggles broke out from the classmates who'd understood.

"Look at her Bucky Beaver teeth," he snickered louder as I pitifully stared at her smiling buck teeth.

We were new to the high school, but we weren't new to unfamiliar surroundings as we'd just spent the past year at a brand new junior high in Port Washington. This would also be her first year as an unassisted teacher, we soon learned. Before coming to Long Island, she'd spent a year in training in Washington, D.C. Before that, she'd been raised in London, England.

She never was what I'd call a good teacher. She may have known her subject inside out, but her downfall was that she played favorites. She only had a few, and they were well spaced among her different classes.

Fortunately for me, I was one of them. I'd never considered myself a teacher's pet; how the hell could that be? All teachers earned their salaries when they had the misfortune of me being assigned to their classes!

But, "Miss T." (we'd compromised) made a deal with me after school one day when she ordered me to stay late.

"You know, you do fine on tests—" she began.

"It comes natural to me," I butted in.

"I know," she continued. "I can see that."

I smiled.

"Of course, you can't spell."

Downcast eyes, and a resigned smile met her light abomination.

"And your sentence structure is occasionally improper."

I continued to shake my head in defeat.

"But you write beautifully, and editors could easily correct your few mistakes."

And I thought to myself, if others can write properly, why would publishers hire me, and an editor to correct my mistakes?

"I'll tell you what I'm going to do, Ronnie; we'll set your desk by a window in the back corner. You just stay there by yourelf, don't listen to me, don't hassle me, or the class. Just scribble one hundred words every day; pick your own subjects. I don't care what you write about, or how your write it. On Fridays, you'll take the same tests as everybody else, which I'm confident you'll pass, then over the weekends, you can put together five hundred words that you can hand in on Monday."

"And that's it?

"That's it," she smiled. "And I'll guarantee you at least a "B" on your report card each marking period."

"Are you talking about for the whole year?" I couldn't believe my ears.

"As long as you don't backslide," she said, showing her first sign of doubt. "But I don't see how you could."

To knock out a dozen or so sentences every day was a snap, I realized. Becauase I love to write, I often wrote hundreds of words for lack of anything better to do.

Well into my writing binge, one day she asked me to come in after school, which I gladly did. She was alone, as expected, but she surprised the hell out of me when I carelessly approached her desk. She looked up, and that's when I saw the tears in her eyes. "Ronnie, you disappoint me horribly."

"What? What'd I do now?" I saw she was serious, and couldn't imagine what was troubling her. She held up the paper I'd turned in a few hours ago. "Why, Ronnie? Why does everything have to be so f...ing big, or so f...ing far, or so f...ing high? I know you have a better vocabulary than that; I hear you talk everyday. Use your mind! There are much better ways to express yourself than using that cheap gutter talk."

She sure knocked the wind from my sails. And since that afternoon many years ago, I haven't been able to curse on paper without thinking of her.

By test time on Fridays, besides having turned in my regular assignments daily, I usually had the writing for that coming weekend complete, too. She liked having a fresh five hundred words to take home for the weekend, and needless to say, I loved tenth grade English.

Then one day she was out sick. A substitute teacher who I'd never laid eyes on took her place. She had my number. I didn't like her, and she didn't like me.

While going through "Miss T's" desk, I later learned, she'd stumbled over a group of my stories. She picked the ones she thought had the best titles, then presented them to the principal.

"Miss T" never came back.

I don't think the principal appreciated my stories with titles like "How to Steal a Boat." I'm sure he didn't feel it was appropriate for a tenth grader to write essays entitled "How to Tap a Keg of Beer," either.

I quit school, and never saw "Miss T" again.

Ronnie Finch

FIFTH AVENUE RUSH HOUR

I STEPPED OFF THE CURB and was standing in the middle of 48th and Fifth when I heard, "Stop him!" as he ran past, tossing the earrings he'd snatched, while the crowd pulled back in on itself like the stomach of a fat man bottled up behind tightly belted pants, pulling back in on itself, chasing uptown after the man, knocking down a woman in a purple dress, as the earrings were gathered up between the treads of a passing taxi, amongst all the beeping and manuvering, they were gathered up and gone, and for awhile, if you were walking downtown, things weren't as compressed or squeezed and you could stick out your arms and not touch anyone, and it was nice, smooth and nice, but you had to walk fast to enjoy it because the crowd began drifting back, like the gradual snapping of overstressed seams on a fat man's pair of pants when the belt has been removed and the stomach released, expanding into the gaps, pressing toward me.

Anonymous

IT'S YOUR WORLD; THE REST OF US JUST LIVE HERE

First, you thought I was all wrong,
    Then all right,
    Again ALRIGHT and
    Finally—just right.

Then it was wrong! Wrong! Wrong!
    Wrong all the way,
    The wrong day and
    No pay.

But you said you didn't really care.
Did I mean it?
Try being mean without it.

Morris Peltz

PARADISE LOST

ON AUGUST 2, THE BRISBANE POLICE accidentally discovered a tramps' paradise when they stumbled upon a small compound of cozy shacks nestled under a tree on unused property between the Southern Pacific tracks near Geneva Avenue, just outside San Francisco city limits.

For the last three years I'd lived there with others in shacks we built which we called home. But the cops declared it illegal and posted an eviction notice which said "We'll be back to tear this down if you don't."

Our presence was known but no one complained. Workers at a nearby lumber company would wave as we bicycled into the city to find food and things to sell.

We had kept the place clean and simple, dug holes for toilets, carried the trash out and hauled in water. My shack had a door and windows, a king–sized bed, wood floor, hibachi and a kerosene lantern. Jars of brown rice, lentils, oatmeal and powdered milk sat on shelves. Books, a radio, and some art made this a real home. There was even a guest house and a sun deck.

But now it's gone and I'm sleeping on the streets. In modern day McDonaldland, we can't build our own houses or sell things on the street without a license. We can't even dig a hole to bury our dead. The system is designed for rich owners to make money, not for people to live good lives.

My name is Bicycle and I think of myself as a gypsy zenster. Riding a bicycle made out of parts found in dumpsters and wearing clothes from free boxes, I have a home–made look that stands out among today's uniforms. I shower at Aquatic Park, City College or at community centers. All my toilet articles come from motel dumpsters. I scavenge abundant fruits and vegetables behind produce stores and under the stalls at the Farmers' Market. I find pizza, sandwich meats, cheese, bread, and even steak and lobster in garbage cans. St. Martin de Porres soup line is my favorite place for delicious soup and good company.

When I was living at the shack, my biggest expense was laundry. Medical problems meant being a guinea pig at General Hospital. I learned that a toothache could be numbed with alcohol until the tooth died in five days.

Some days I'd get a day's work, but my favorite way to spend the day was hiking on San Bruno Mountain or taking sightseeing rides on my bicycle, sometimes taking an overnight ride up north.

These past summers and winters, when I rode out to that quiet green field or lay inside my shack, warm and dry during a rain storm, or sat next to an evening campfire, I got strong sexual feelings. I'd take off my clothes first thing when I got back to the shack. Freedom is the strongest aphrodisiac.

At night I had to sleep under mosquito netting made from curtain backing. Moonlight would come through the windows and screech owls screamed in the dark. Spiders occasionally dropped from the ceiling. Lizards, jack rabbits, squirrels and even weasles and fox lived nearby. Sometimes stray dogs wandered in but nothing was ever stolen because it was so well hidden.

But by chance the cops stumbled onto it and now it's all gone. When I returned a few weeks later, I found the shacks chain–sawed down and strewn all over.

Bicycle

AMERICA

America is the most richest and powerful country in the world
Especially if you happen to be of a minority race
All of our freedom fighters here in America
Are either refugees from other countries
Or else they are people born here but happen to be of a minority race
I mysef am a refugee in the country of my birth.

James English

A STALE DONUT

PASSING

HENRIETTA STOOD WITH OTHER CRAMMED PEOPLE at the back of the third car of the N Judah train during one of the city's late evening rush hours, holding the hand rail, shifting, searching for a seat. She was not one to allow a jammed train to prevent her from sitting and quickly hunched forward when she saw an elderly woman pull the buzzer wire and slowly begin to rise. Henrietta moved in closer to the woman's seat, pushing, squeezing immediately behind her rising rump as she half stood, Sister give me time and I'll be out of your way! and sat down accomplished in an aisle seat. Looking out the window, Henrietta watched the passing lights and skyscrapers balloon and shrink weaving through the reflection of her face and she considered, It is my reflection these lights and buildings are trying to get into. Mine.

When the N Judah drew into the next stop, the small rectangular lights within the train shut off and Henrietta's reflection disappeared into the now stably dominant skyline. Henrietta stood to leave, stumbling over her feet as the faceless rush of the exiting crowd shoved her out. She swayed behind a thick warning yellow line at the edge of the station platform, holding her space against the jostling of others, waiting for the J Train to arrive and take her the remainder of the way into the city. A man's elbow snapped into her face and she jerked back, cupping her hands over her face, as several frantic feet scuffed into her spot.

The doors of the N Judah hissed closed. Henrietta and everyone surrounding her leaned with the train as it started its steady thrust forward. Gaining momentum, the cars of the train smeared by in gray blurs, blending into one another as the speed increased, increased, increased, becoming indistinguishably one until there was only a hollow windy sound echoing up from the tracks, and Henrietta, not one to allow herself to be pooped out of the way, rolled impatiently against the crowd, heel to ball, heel to ball, waiting, vying for position.

Anonymous

A PUNCH IS AS . . .

A punch is as good as a kiss,
An unwashed sonata of vagrant dreams,
Immobile, yet mobilized,
Painfully silent
Ecstatically berserk.

Oh, God, that ever did human grace
Give man such trammeled care,
To feel that pierce, that plunge,
The softness,
That sharp, spear–like thrust,
To void the pill of pleasing lassitude.

Capture irony, freeze anomaly.
Pale the dots of seamless,
Yet infernal agony
And make bloom again, lush and verdant,
The entrails of timeless hesitance.

Break out, get broken into.
Farm out the lazy
Band of extraneous verdure.
Get with it, man!
Or else, be prepared
For endless hopelessness.

Morris Peltz

JOHN DOE, MAT 9

TODAY I AM DOCILE

I once was a killer
of stately enemies
I once was a writer
of protest songs;
Today I am docile
Tomorrow I'll rule
with a fistful of passion
in a country of fools.

Serenity lives
near the Golden Gate Bridge
in the bay in the mist;
As in Otis's song—
Today it is morning
the foghorns rejoice
calling to one another
they share in a voice.

I make all my rounds
without leaving a trace
and sit by the water,
the breeze in my face;
The future is distant
yet triumph is near
I notice the sounds
only spirits can hear.

There's a bottle of rum
laying firmly at hand
and it's whispering softly
so I'll understand
that its magic is subtle
its powers sublime;
it's there for my pleasure,
its poetry shines.

To cast pearls in the ocean
is all very fine
To plant trees in an orchard
is fineness in kind;
Today I am docile
tomorrow I'll rule,
with a fistful of passion
in a kingdom of fools.

Seth Richardson

KRIS

WHAT IS THROWN EMPIRE AND ARMIES OF GLORY, blood–stained streamers and a word which cracks enemy battlements like so much chalk.

The girl, my exquisite girl, how much was she to me? Her eyes were so inviting, her lips just pursed, and her form ballet to the trained eye, and my eyes were trained on her and her alone. For years I longed to kiss her, to be loved by her. At night I would lay my tired body and mind into my bed. Closing my eyes I would press my face into her warm yet unloved image.

Tired, yes, I was tired, my body would ache from the day's labors, and the mind would go blank from books to many books. A warrior's prize she was, my jewel in a long phrophesied war. What happened to Kris and her champion? I fell with her. Her loss was my greatest, next in pain was my loss of her and finally the rest.

So pile the gold high light a mountain of dead men. What is it worth? And empire, what is empire but kingdoms, kingdoms but dust! Isn't it said that from dust we come and to dust we return?

Of fame now I speak: Tis better for a man to hear the sweet cooing of one's beloved in one's ear, than the shrill cry from a world of sirens. Sirens that know you not, see you not and love even less.

Finally, the crown, oh, yes, let me tell you something of the crown. Heavy is the king's crown and all too often hard and cold is the metal. Believe me not! Then here is your test, man. Some night when your heart aches and tears spill uncontrolled, touch the woman who loves you dear, caress the breast that nurses you.

Now with your right hand, please, the sword hand, for all worthy crowns are taken by the sword. Touch that crown of cold metal and crystal. Does this hard one soothe you or comfort you as you whimper in your sleep? I say it cannot.

In my fooled imagination I once had a choice between a girl or an empire of dust and birds of prey. I valued her more than all the earth. I loved more then the host of heaven. For this to punish me, struck she was and with her cast down I was as a seraph with burned wings. In my encompassing void I miss her. Mostly I miss what never was.

Hard was my fall to earth. Even now much of what once was reels. What has happened? I thirst for her. Great is my thirst, though I drink not. On the day I die is there really a God in heaven? Is there really a lord of host? If so, I challenge *you*! When it is my time, let it be quick. I am no longer great. My crown is now dust. If you are truly a God of mercy, let my last hour be in the golden season. Give me one hour for what would have been. Is there anything now, save the stone!

Edward Alexander

CONVERSATIONS

MARSIE (WHICH STARTED OUT AS MY BEST FRIEND) LEFT TOWN never to speak to me any more. I miss her very much, but I screwed that up because while she was in the hospital having a baby, I was having an affair with her husband while taking care of her family for her; not much of a friend was I? Later, I had a son by him; she found out and that took care of that. Joe now lives with my father. I'm afraid I'm not much of a mother either. I should be with him and be able to take care of him, but I have trouble enough taking care of myself.

Elaine was my second best friend. She was killed in a car accident (she didn't die right away, instead she had terrible pain for three solid months). It really was tragic because she had left town with her boyfriend and his father to get married. I went along for moral support, and we were all drinking, as usual, having a great time, when out of the clear blue we were run off the road by another drunk driver. I was thrown clear (what dumb, stupid luck) but she was pinned under the car. Her boyfriend and his father were killed instantly. Now, get the picture, when I left to get help (which for some unknown reason I didn't make it back, but the police did), she did have on rings and watches (boyfriend and father, too) and a pair of bright red, new shoes. They were found minus those items when the police arrived. Someone had the nerve to stop and steal from them, and left them to die—I call that inhuman. After that I tried not to make many friends, the only other friend and love I had was Frank, he means a great deal to me today and always holds a special place in my heart.

I have so many things I'd like to write, that it would take me a week just to write everything I have ever done. I'm sorry for acting like a fool, no one twisted my arm to drink, I played that part all by myself; it's not hard being a fool, but being able to admit I'm wrong in why I do these things, I can own up to my mistakes. It might take some doing, but I know I'm wrong when I think that only problem consists from drinking because it doesn't. I will admit I do have emotional problems I can't handle by myself and I just try and convince myself that a drink will take care of it, but it only seems to make the matter worse.

By the way, I used to be good, for six years steady I went to church and sang in the choir. I wonder where I messed up.

Well, here I sit thinking of the past again. It really is an experience to run through my life. I've done so many things, it would take a year to write about them. When I worked at the bar (Silver Dollar) I was always considered the best worker. That's where I met Alvin. I didn't like him when I first met him. I thought he was a snob. He'd buy me drinks and take me to dinner, just to see how long it would take him to get me into bed. I finally gave in, but it was fun to tease him, at the time, anyway. We grew to be a twosome and sometimes Frank would go out with us. Were were all great friends. We spent a great deal of time together, the only problem I had was trying to stay sober long enough to do my work. Finally, one morning when the boss came in, I was sitting there drinking my usual beer with a guy I knew real well (Joe) at 6 a.m. Don asked me if I was going to be able to work that night and I said yes. I mean, after all, all I had was two beers. Well lunch time comes around and here I still sit in the same place (different guys, of course) and certainly different drinks, and my boss asks again if I'm sure I'll be able to work. Yes, I'm not drunk yet. Well, you guessed it, comes 3 p.m. and by that time I had to agree to take the night off. I was well on the way. Back then, I drank mostly white port wine, my favorite. Now it would probably kill me. Anyway, I must have enjoyed myself, I remember Frank and I going to dinner and then back to the bar. After that, I'm at a complete loss, as I had a blackout spell. The people at the bar said I drove Frank's car out to Don's house and gave him the bar key and told him to shove the job. Of course, I can't remember. So the next day was Saturday and I needed a drink very badly. Frank and I headed for the bar about 7 a.m., had a couple of drinks (whiskey sours), and found out that the night before I had quit my job. Don said he thought it was for the best since it was bad for my health.

Anonymous

PERSONAL NOTES, ETC.

I seek the dreams
of rainbow queens
on blanket streets
in rainy times
The air is mellow
in its way
a high of substance
that is mine.

Seth Richardson

SIN CITY, U.S.A.

You meet the pimps and whores
riding in Fleetwoods and Rolls
the true–true fakers and the real money–makers
You meet the winoes and the hypes
with their wine bottles and spikes
and the slick sweet macks
and the smooth talking players
along with high–sider, low–rider, boosters,
pick–pockets, soothesayers and
thieves, dope dealers and whore
houses beyond your belief.
Yes, this is the city, Sin City, U.S.A.,
San Francisco, CA

Weldon Kennedy

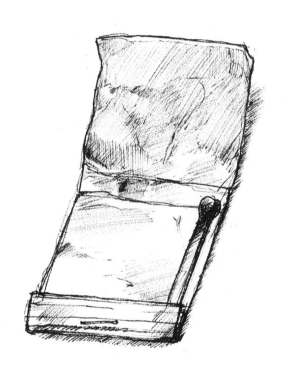

THANKSGIVING

A crust of bread and a corner to sleep in
A minute to smile and an hour to weep in
A peck of gay and a pound of trouble
Never any happiness but the moans come double
So, give thanks for what?

James English

"COFFEE BREAK"

CONRAD '86

OUT OF THE RAIN

Out of the rain and into your hearts—
    Such an easy thing to say.
We look and think we feel.
    We act and think we care.

Such a motley crew that homeless crowd is—
    Anyway.
Derelicts of one description or another—
    hardly worth mentioning.

Do you think, if God had cared,
    they would be where they are?
Or, indeed, is this their punishment
    for some prior grievous error?

I wish I knew some of these answers,
    For then I could act with clarity.
And then with all that clarity
    Charity itself wouldn't seem so far away.

Morris Peltz

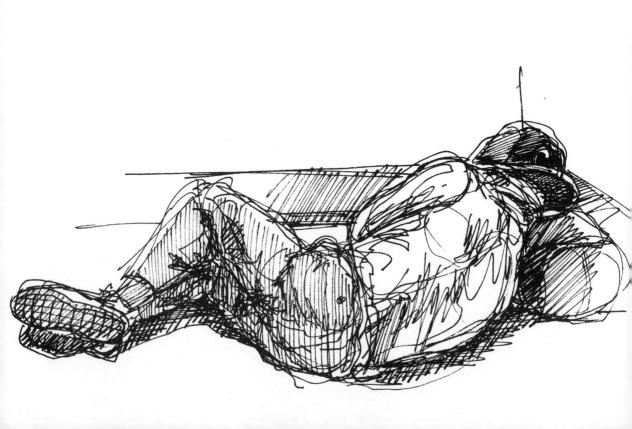